The OCEAN Alphabet Book

by Jerry Pallotta
Illustrated by Frank Mazzola, Jr.

 Charlesbridge

Published by
Charlesbridge Publishing
85 Main Street
Watertown, MA 02472
(617) 926-0329
www.charlesbridge.com

Library of Congress Cataloging-in-Publication Data
Pallotta, Jerry.
    The ocean alphabet book / by Jerry Pallotta; Frank Mazzola, Jr.,
illustrator.
        p.   cm.
    Summary: Introduces the letters A to Z by describing fish and other
creatures living in the North Atlantic Ocean.
    ISBN 0-88106-458-0 (reinforced for library use)
    ISBN 0-88106-452-1 (softcover)
    1. Marine fauna—Juvenile literature. 2. English language—Alphabet
—Juvenile literature.
[1. Marine animals. 2. Alphabet.] I. Mazzola, Frank, ill. II. Title.
QL122.2.P35   1991
591.92 — dc20
                                                            89-60424
                                                            CIP
                                                            AC

Printed in the United States of America
(sc) 25 24 23 22 21 20
(hc) 10 9 8 7

Printed on Recycled Paper

Books by Jerry Pallotta:
The Icky Bug Alphabet Book
The Icky Bug Counting Book
The Bird Alphabet Book
The Flower Alphabet Book
The Yucky Reptile Alphabet Book
The Frog Alphabet Book
The Furry Animal Alphabet Book
The Dinosaur Alphabet Book
The Underwater Alphabet Book
The Victory Garden Vegetable Alphabet Book
The Extinct Alphabet Book
The Desert Alphabet Book
The Spice Alphabet Book
The Butterfly Alphabet Book
The Freshwater Alphabet Book
The Airplane Alphabet Book
The Boat Alphabet Book
The Jet Alphabet Book
Going Lobstering
Dory Story
Cuenta los insectos (The Icky Bug Counting Book)
The Crayon Counting Book
The Crayon Counting Board Book

This book is dedicated to Nicholas and Jeffrey Pallotta.

Aa

A is for Alphabet Book.
A is also for Atlantic Ocean. The fish and other creatures in this book live in the North Atlantic Ocean.

B b B is for Bluefish. Everyone loves to catch Bluefish because they love to fight. Their teeth are very, very sharp, so don't ever put your fingers in their mouths.

C c

C is for Cod. Cod can be found everywhere in the North Atlantic Ocean. Some grow to be as big as a ten-year-old boy or girl.

D d

D is for Dogfish. They are also known as Spiny Dogfish. They are little sharks. Every Dogfish has a barb on its back and a barb on its tail.

E e

E is for Eel. Eels are slimy! Eels are long and thin like snakes. If you do not like to hold snakes, then you probably would not like to hold Eels.

F f

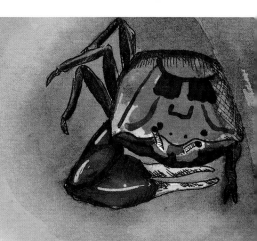

F is for Fiddler Crab. Most crabs have claws that are the same size. The Fiddler Crab has one big claw and one tiny claw.

G is for Goosefish. A Goosefish is ugly-looking. It has lots of teeth. Its mouth is as wide as its body. Goosefish are also called monkfish.

Gg

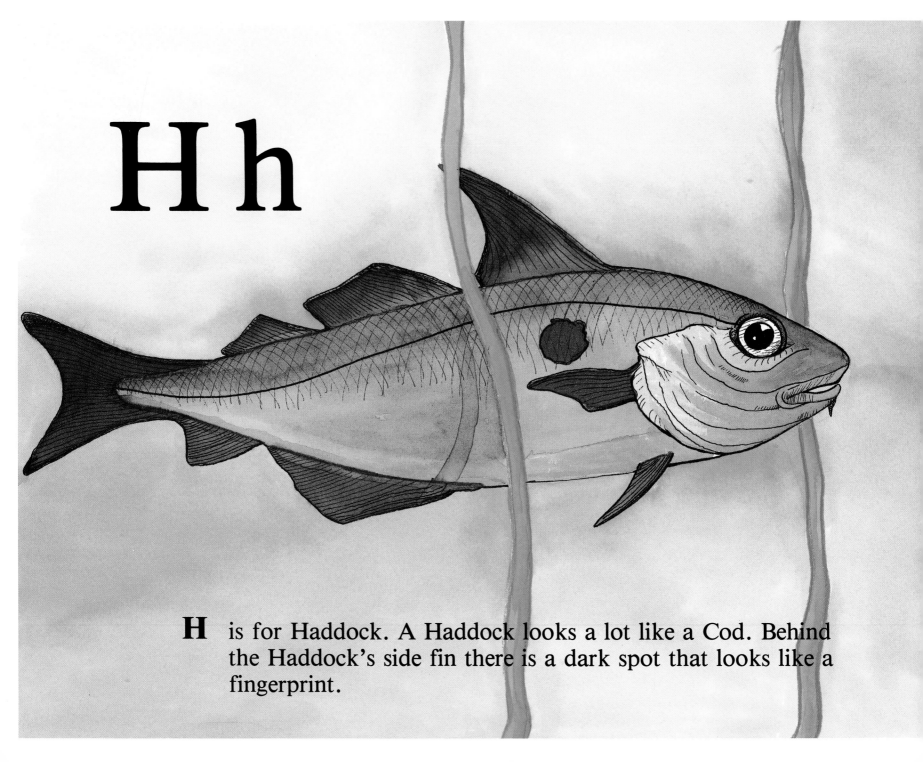

H h

H is for Haddock. A Haddock looks a lot like a Cod. Behind the Haddock's side fin there is a dark spot that looks like a fingerprint.

I i

I is for Ink. Ink is not the name of a fish. Squid spray ink to scare away fish that attack them.

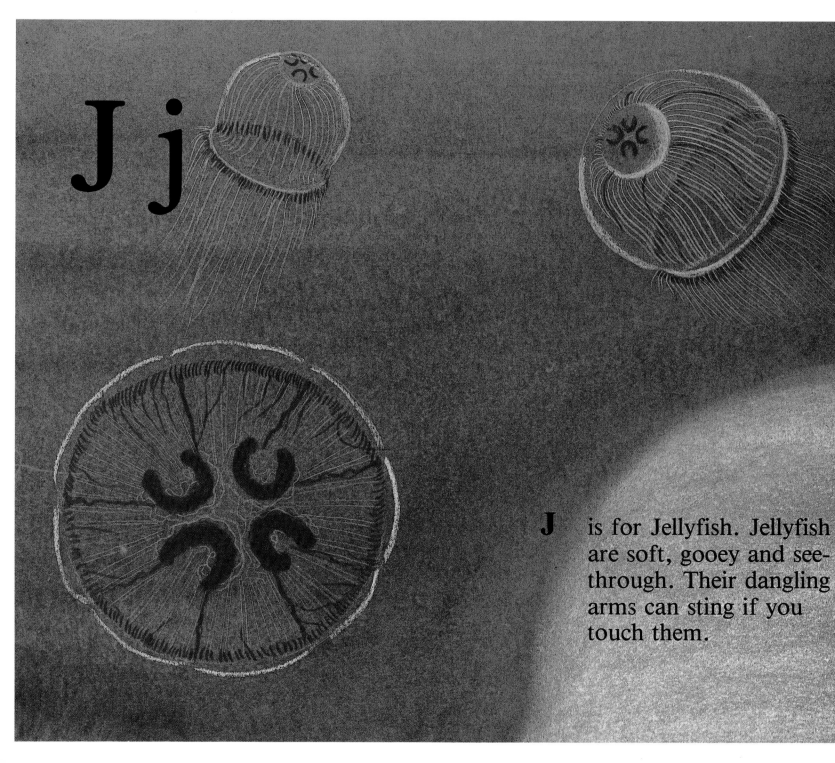

J j

J is for Jellyfish. Jellyfish are soft, gooey and see-through. Their dangling arms can sting if you touch them.

K is for Killer Whale. Killer Whales are mammals. They are not fish. They are very beautiful and can jump completely out of the water.

Kk

L l

L is for Lobster. Lobsters are reddish-green and blue. When they are cooked they turn bright red. They have two claws that can pinch. They have eight legs. They also have two antennas that help them find out where they are.

Mm

M is for Minnow. Minnows are little fish. Usually they are only as big as your fingers. They can be found in shallow waters, marshlands and creeks.

Nn

N is for Northern Puffer. If you touch a Puffer, it will blow itself up like a balloon.

O o

O is for Octopus. This Octopus is scary-looking, but it will not hurt you. It has eight arms. Can you imagine shaking hands with an Octopus? It would take all day!

Pp

P is for Periwinkle. Periwinkles live inside shells. They can be found on rocks at low tide. Some people call them snails.

Q q

Q is for Quahog. Quahogs are clams that have hard shells. Seagulls manage to open them all by themselves. Small Quahogs are called cherrystones and littlenecks.

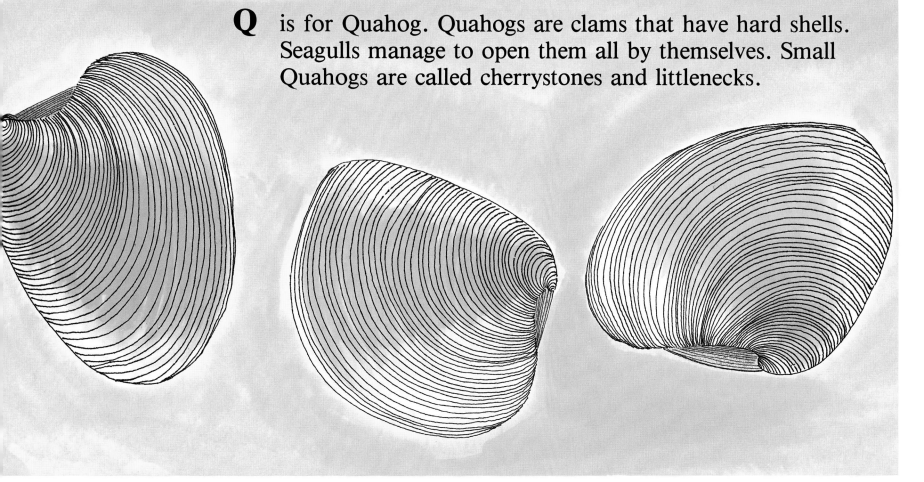

Rr

R is for Redfish. Redfish are caught in very deep water. They are oily, and lobstermen use them as bait to catch lobsters.

S s

S is for Scallop. Scallops are like clams, and they have pretty shells. There are many other creatures whose names begin with S: Sharks, Sculpins, Salmon, Sand Dollars, Sunfish, Smelt, Sea Snails, Skates, Shrimp and Starfish.

T t

T is for Tuna. Everybody has heard of Tuna.
When they are grown-up, they are almost as
big as cars.

Uu

U is for Urchin. Urchins are round with hundreds of sharp little spines sticking out of their shells. If you are barefoot, try not to step on one!

V v

V is for Viperfish. Viperfish live in deep, dark waters. They have lights inside their mouths and along their sides to attract food.

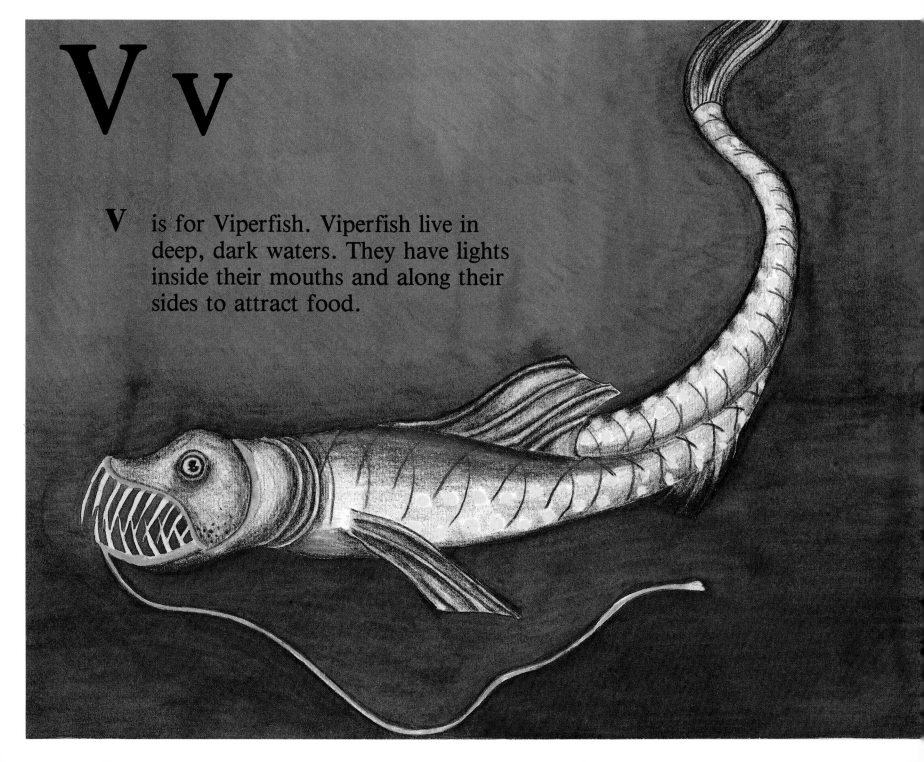

W w

W is for Wolffish. Wolffish have large teeth and strong jaws that are used to open their favorite foods: quahogs, scallops, clams and mussels.

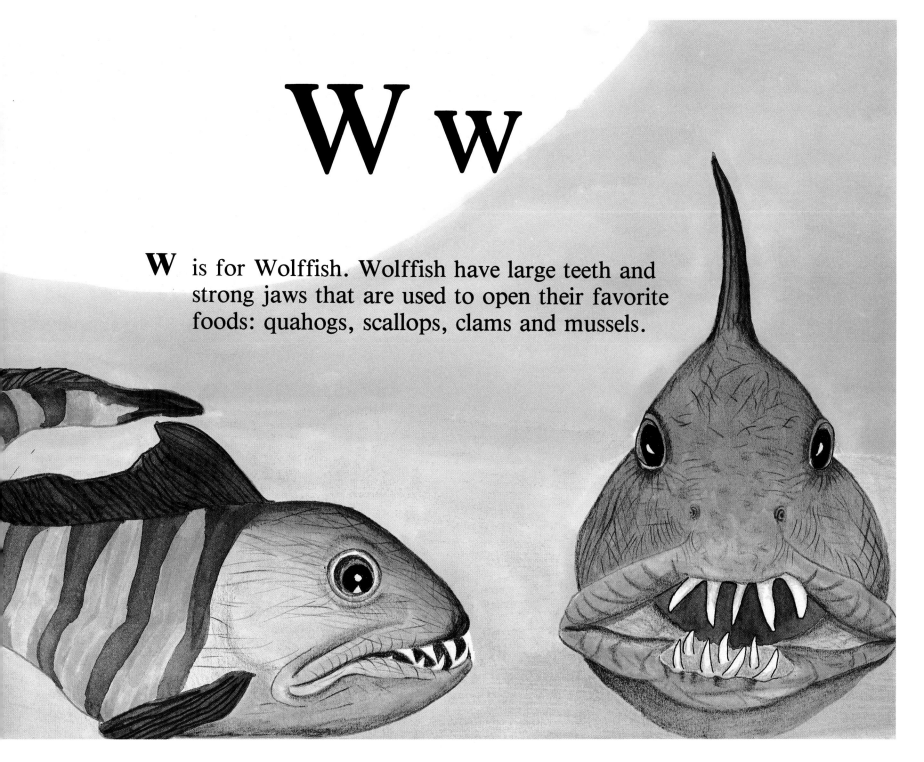

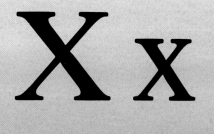

X x

We cannot think of any fish whose names begin with the letter **X**! Can you?

Xx

Oops, we found one! **X** is for Xiphias gladius (pronounced — Ziphias). This is the scientific name for Swordfish.

Y is for Yellow-tail Flounder. Yellow-tails are flat fish with both eyes on one side of their heads. They are called Yellow-tails because their tails are yellow.

Yy

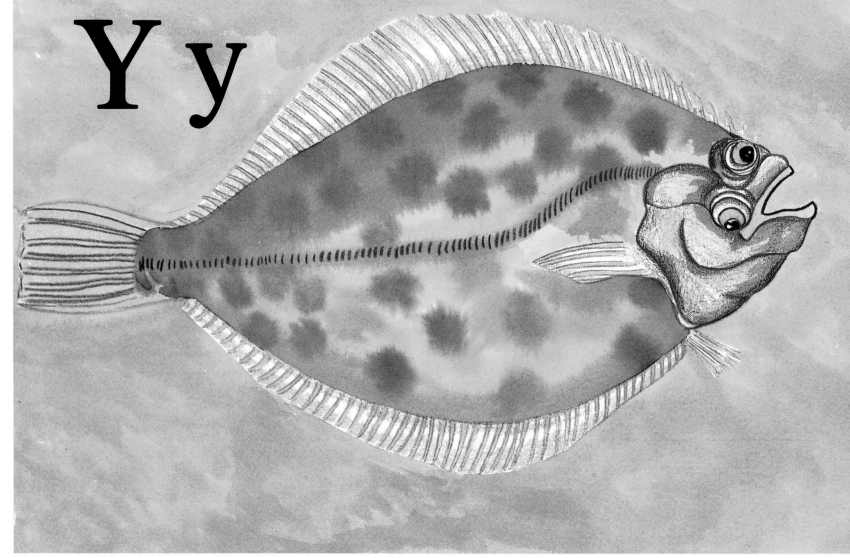

Z z

Z is for Zillions. That's how many fish there are in the ocean!